A
JOYFUL
SOUL

00 01 02 03 04 RDR 10 9 8 7 6 5 4 3 2 1

Library of Congress Cataloging-in-Publication Data

John XXIII, Pope, 1881–1963.
    A joyful soul : messages from a saint for our times / Pope John XXIII ; edited by Jerome M. Vereb.
        p. cm.
    ISBN 0-7407-1018-4 (hardcover)
    1. Spiritual life—Catholic Church—Quotations, maxims, etc. 2. Holiness—Catholic Church—Quotations, maxims, etc. I. Vereb, Jerome M. II. Title.

BX2350.2.J57 2000
282'.092—dc21   00-030555

Book design by Lisa Martin
Printed in Mexico

A
JOYFUL
SOUL

Messages from a Saint for Our Times

POPE JOHN XXIII

Edited by Jerome M. Vereb, C.P.

A Giniger Book
Published in association with

**Andrews McMeel
Publishing**

Kansas City

To the memory of

Anne Gallagher Ferguson

1929–1997

Contents

Foreword

It is a great honor and even a triumph for me to put my name in this book, as it presents the spirituality given to the world by Pope John XXIII. I still remain enchanted by the charisma of simplicity shining on the face of this Pope who came from our Italian countryside.

It is moreover a chance to thank the American people, who have the merit of having opened their curtains, according to the prophetic omen, to welcome men and women coming from every origin and culture: "Let the curtains of your habitations be stretched out; do not hold back, lengthen your cords and strengthen your stakes. For you will spread out to the right and to the left" (Isa 54:2–3).

John XXIII regretted not having ever set foot in America, a vast territory that nevertheless became part of his apostolic charity. Friends abroad will be pleased to know his comment to the letter, addressed to me on February 21, 1963, by Robert Blair Kaiser, of *Time* magazine. He asked me about the possibility of the Pope's taking a trip to New York to "participate in a dinner for all persons who have ever appeared on the cover of *Time*." I expected the Pope to deal with it with a smile or a formal note. Instead, without a blush, he wrote a message that was an unmistakable sign of his ability to adjust to the times and to a modern mentality without feeling tied to protocol: "Nothing can be against a project that sooner or later will have to be accepted. But too many other circumstances are needed for it to happen."

This book, *A Joyful Soul: Messages from a Saint for Our Times*, edited by Jerome M. Vereb, appears like the realization of John XXIII's visit to the United States, where he surely comes with his love and pastoral care.

There were countless messages sent to the Catholics abroad to encourage their ventures and to thank them for the support shown toward the needy, while urging further pastoral, catechetical, missionary, and social commitments.

Pope John still turns to all Christians, as before him his predecessors and after him his successors, in confirming the vocations, the activities, and the merits. He was aware of human fragility and temptations. He also knew that apart from the divine law there is a genuine foreboding regarding the achievements of civilizations, and of progress and the accomplishment of solidarity and the universal brotherhood.

Once again, Pope John places on the lips of the generous sons and daughters abroad words that he pronounced at the beginning of his pontificate: "I am your brother Joseph" (Gen 45:4) and "The entire world is my family" (August 15, 1959).

In the light of the beatification of Elizabeth Ann Seton, the first American-born citizen ever elevated to the honor of canonization, Pope John acknowledged America's virtue in the context of its history and the specificity of its call to a steadfastness of faith, to a passion of charity, and to a joyful satisfaction of vocation. He said: "In the United States, to those heroes of the most noble human feats, in life and death, applause and love. It is a pleasure to acknowledge that respect and love are awake in men and women devoted to Christ, to his gospel, to assistance carried out in an evangelical spirit, and also to the most rigid ascetic discipline, in the increasing growth of meditative orders. American citizens have ploughed the seas and skies, accomplished excellent feats, given great hospitality and work to men coming from every corner of the earth. America has continued to courageously overcome, from era to era, the subsequent difficulties, while giving . . . legislation that descends from the principles of moral Christianity, a substance that satisfies the dignity of human beings. It gives us much comfort to bear witness to the prominent nation, hoping for a rush of spiritual success."

This simple book, which Father Vereb places in the hands of teachers, could be defined as the vade mecum of evangelical simplicity: that state of mind that presumes that human and Christian virtues are assembled together to help mankind grow within the dimensions of dignity and goodness of the disciple of Christ. Recall the short prayer that was written by Pope John on March 17, 1963: "O blessed Elizabeth Seton, who today shines before all the nations for the faith shown in the baptismal promises, look over your people with compassion; they rejoice with you as the first flower of sanctity. Obtain the grace from God to keep the ed patrimony of the gospel's call, the steadfastness of faith, and the passion of charity, until it joyfully satisfies its vocation."

The following comprehensive prayer, taken from Pope John's patrimony, could inspire the readers of this book to continue the invocation on September 3 of the 2000 Jubilee year, the day of his beatification:

"Blessed Pope John, we give thanks to the Holy Trinity for having sent you to us, loving brother and wise master.

"You have climbed the Mount of the Beatitudes, letting yourself be led in all things and always by divine providence, from boyhood in a country farmhouse in Sotto il Monte until you became a bishop of the universal Church.

"Ask the Father of every consolation for the grace for us to welcome the Good Tidings and to remain steadfast in the impenetrable faith, in the indestructible hope of charity without limits; to accept blissful and blessed poverty; to silently serve with perseverance; to desire heavenly goods and to break away from earthly goods, so as to open our minds to the needs of the Church and contemporary humanity. To give us the wisdom of the heart to love all as brothers, to forgive and embrace the errant, to favor the breaking of barriers in the misunderstandings between men and

peoples, to suppress selfishness and to prompt the fertile unity of the spirits.

"Supported by our heavenly Mother, we will particularly be intent on the name, the kingdom, and the will of God. Humility and mildness will shine on our faces. We will understand that justice and goodness consist in remaining, like the saints, in a spiritual childhood, which grows little by little according to our own particular vocation.

"Through Christ our Lord. Amen."

LORIS CAPOVILLA
Archbishop of Nesembria

Sotto il Monte Giovanni XXIII, Italy
April 22, 2000

Introduction

⟞⟞⟞⟞

Sometime in June 1960, Father Malcolm LaVelle, then General Superior of the Passionists, was received in private audience by Pope John XXIII. The purpose of the visit was to discuss the development of overseas missions, especially in Latin America. While the interview itself was short, at the conclusion of the conversation the American priest offered a letter that he had promised to pass on to the Pontiff on behalf of a fellow religious. Pope John opened the letter right then and there and began to read it in the presence of his guest. At the end of the reading, the Pope sighed and said, "People have such hard lives . . . too many problems . . . so many temptations . . . such struggle!"

"And you, Holy Father, how do you do it?" queried Father Malcolm. "Surely yours must be the hardest life of all? So much responsibility! How do you sleep at night?"

"Oh, I sleep very well," replied Pope John. "Every night, I kneel at the prie-dieu in my room and wash my thoughts and my sins in the blood of Jesus. I see myself dropping them one by one into the chalice. By dawn, when I rise, I know they are clean. I live in the confidence of the meaning of the Redemption, and it makes me very happy. I get up refreshed every morning, not only from sleep but from the drops of medicine that come only from the Cross."

All during the rest of Father LaVelle's life he treasured that relationship with Pope John and the memory of that late conversation. Above all, as he recalled to me years later, he was aware precisely of the quality of holiness with which Pope John XXIII had endowed the Church. It was the Pontiff's sense of absolute confidence in the ways of God: "These are not often comprehensible and the environment of this age is rarely up to our ideals and expectations, but this *is* God's world and the events *are* God's affairs. It is therefore *God's* task to bring us through even our own disappointments and disillusions. To love him ultimately means to trust God absolutely."

John XXIII was, even in his lifetime, called "Good Pope John." He was widely beloved for his spontaneity, tenderness, simplicity, and honesty. These qualities are the components of his holiness. In Rome, a city that is always critical of its popes, John's picture today hangs in houses, businesses, sports arenas, coffee bars, and ordinary cars. As one taxi driver told me only the other day, pointing to his medallion: "I pray to him every day. Why? Because he is an honest man!" The Pope's goodness rests on that fact.

Throughout his entire life, the Angelo Roncalli who was destined to become Pope John XXIII took seriously the call to holiness. Under Jesuit, Redemptorist, Franciscan, and Passionist spiritual directors, he attempted to reach a point of personal simplicity where God could act in him for his own sanctification and for the good of his ministry to the Church and for the world. The elements of that simplicity, according to his own words, are

patience, gentleness, and affability. The dynamic of that simplicity is the faith that "God is doing something in me even though I do not see it or feel it!"

Pope John, quite early on, recognized Saint John Vianney, the Curé of Ars (1786–1859), as a special patron saint for the whole of his ministry. He dedicated one of his eight encyclicals, *Sacerdotii Nostri Primordia,* to the memory of this mid-nineteenth-century parish priest from France. He often quoted him, especially about the dignity and sacramental power of a priest's hands. But his favorite phrase concerned his own personal core. "Humility is like a balance," he cited: "the more one lowers himself on the one side, the higher he raises himself on the other." Pope John repeated this maxim as he made a midday and evening examination of conscience. Historians and ecclesiologists of the future will evaluate John XXIII's pontificate highly for its ecumenical and conciliar legacy, as well as for his sense of the political and economic arena of twentieth-century globalization. At this time of his beatification on September 3, 2000, however, the entire Church claims as precious the memory and lessons of his valiantly simple heart.

Pope John made his retreat for priestly ordination at the

Passionist monastery of Saints John and Paul in Rome, where I currently reside. During these spiritual exercises, he was impressed by the piety and simplicity of a young Spaniard named Eugene Viso, known in religion as Brother Thomas of the Passion. Throughout his ten days of silence, Deacon Angelo Roncalli was served at table by Brother Thomas. He also observed Brother Thomas in prayer, prostrate on bare ground before the reserved Eucharist in the monastery chapel. This scene inspired the seminarian to ask God for the graces of penitence, humility, modesty, prayerfulness, and true wisdom. He wrote: "Ah, Brother Thomas, what a lot I am learning from you! So many of these humble, little lay brothers, so many unknown religious, will one day shine with glory in the Kingdom of Heaven. And why should not I too shine? O Jesus, give me the spirit of penitence, sacrifice, and mortification." The words of Pope John, as found in this book, coupled with the drama and the humor of his pontificate, are surely proof that the Lord heard his prayer on the eve of his priestly ordination.

This little volume contains some of the thoughts of Pope John derived from his encyclicals, his family letters, his journal, his devotional homilies, and his retreat resolutions. These words

are intended to provide, through his maxims, an insight into his understanding of the holiness he felt called to embody. More specifically, they are intended to bring comfort to all at the inception of the twenty-first century.

JEROME M. VEREB, C.P.

Monastery of SS. John and Paul, Rome, Italy
Passionist Congregation
Feast of the Annunciation
March 25, 2000

Commitment to Jesus the Christ

———— ∞∞∞ ————

*Throughout his life,
no matter where he was,
Pope John always insisted on making
the Ignatian spiritual exercises annually.
The theme of absolute discipleship to
Christ constantly remains at the core
of his personal spirituality. It is found in
his diaries and official statements alike.*

$\mathscr{S}$aint Ignatius desires to see the effort to
acquire a virtue even more than the virtue itself.
We must cultivate detachment from all created things.

What have I done for Christ?
Little, little or nothing.
What am I doing for Christ?
Something, but badly, like a sluggard.
What should I do for Christ?
Everything, O Lord, if you do but help
me with your holy grace.

We know that God has given us a mind capable of discovering the law of nature (the gospel). If we follow this, we follow God himself, the Author of that law and the Guide and Director of our lives. If because of foolishness or laziness, or even because of some moral turpitude, we turn our backs on it, we turn our backs on the highest good and the only suitable directive of right living.

THE DUTY OF EVERY CHRISTIAN IS TO
"STRIVE FIRST FOR THE KINGDOM OF GOD" (MT 6:33).

Everything else will be given to us in superabundance
in a life that is honored, civilized, tranquil, and law-abiding.
Those who are unfamiliar with the gospel find the truth
hard to admit; indeed, they laugh it to scorn, and pity
the faithful Christian. We must disillusion them, and
show them the highest dignity and the richest and truest
rewards are won by fidelity to the teaching of the gospel.

$\mathcal{B}$ut above all and in all things
I must endeavor to express in my inner life
and outward behavior the image of Jesus,
"gentle and lowly of heart." May God help me.

$\mathcal{L}$ove is all; love is the foundation
of civilization; love is the basis of all Christ
came to declare to the world.

It is the command to love that distinguishes
the Christian revelation from the doctrine of all
other religions. In love is found the solution
of all social problems, of all political disputes.
It is the keystone of the Church.

*C*hristianity is not that complex system of
oppressive rules that the unbeliever describes;
it is peace, joy, love, and a life that is continually renewed,
like the mysterious pulse of nature at
the beginning of spring. We must assert this
truth . . . must be convinced of it—for it is
your greatest treasure, which alone can give
meaning and serenity to your daily life.

$\mathcal{O}$ur appeal for unity is intended as an echo
of the prayer that our Savior addressed to his
Divine Father at the Last Supper: "That they all may
be one. As you, Father, are in me and I am in you,
may they also be in us." There is no doubt about the
fulfillment of this prayer, just as the cruel sacrifice of
Golgotha was fulfilled. Did the Lord not say that his
Father always hears him? We then believe that the
Church for which he prayed and for which he sacrificed
himself on the cross, and to which he promised his
abiding presence, has always been and remains one,
holy, catholic, and apostolic, just as it was instituted.

First of all, we must have faith in God,
without whose assistance it is impossible to achieve
any lasting success even in the material world. . . .
Faith in God, then, but also faith in yourselves,
in the wonderful powers God has given to
every man for the development of his personality,
in his chosen way of life.

This is the mission of the Church, catholic and apostolic: to reunite men whom selfishness and disillusionment might keep apart, to show them how to pray, to bring them to contrition for their sins and to forgiveness, to feed them with the Eucharistic Bread, and to bind them together with the bonds of charity.

When we fall we must at once repent, rise again, and try not to fall again, and always rejoice in the Lord, thinking of him, looking to him.

$\mathcal{I}$t is not just ordinary mercy that is needed here. The burden of social and personal wickedness is so grave that an ordinary gesture of love does not suffice for forgiveness. So we invoke the great mercy.

$\mathcal{J}$ust as Jesus Christ immolated himself, so his minister ought to immolate himself together with him. Just as Jesus Christ expiated the sins of men, so the priest, by the lofty road of the Christian ascetic life, must attain to the purification of himself and of his neighbors.

*I*t is commonly believed and considered
fitting that even the everyday language of the
Pope should be full of mystery and awe.
But the example of Jesus is more closely followed
in the most appealing simplicity, not dissociated from
the God-given prudence of wise and holy men!

∞

*W*e urgently exhort all our children in every part
of the world, whether clergy or laity, that they fully
understand how great is the nobility and dignity they
derive from being joined to Christ, as branches to
the vine—as he himself said: "I am the Vine,
you are the branches" (Jn 15:5)—and that they
are sharers in his divine life.

∞

The general character of my resolutions of these days is expressed in the simple words of *The Imitation of Christ,* "Desire to be unknown, and little esteemed." But with this, I must never lose heart. On the contrary, I must always be cheerful, serene, and courageous, until my last hour.

I know that you trust the Lord and feel ready for anything. This is the only way. Confidence in the Lord and a brave heart will be your protection and salvation. The Lord does not like fearful men. He is with those who try to be brave and patient at all times.

The gospel contains the fullness of holiness. It presents it to us in the most attractive light, gently tempered to our frail sight. It means simplicity, purity of heart, and humility, even welcoming insults and rejoicing in suffering, forgiving offenses, showing charity to our enemies, with forgetfulness of self and self-denial. In short, it is all that is most directly opposed to the faulty inclinations of our nature, all that most resembles and most nearly approaches the divine perfection.

The Lord Jesus, the founder of Holy Church, directs all that happens with wisdom, power, and indescribable goodness according to his own pleasure and for the greater good of his elect who form his Church, his beloved mystical bride.

If we look on the dignity of the human person in the light of divinely revealed truth, we cannot help but esteem it far more highly; for men are redeemed by the blood of Jesus Christ—they are by grace the children and friends of God and heirs of eternal glory.

$\mathcal{I}$t is natural that the souls created by God
and destined for eternal life should seek to discover
the truth, the primary object of the human mind's
activity. Why must we speak the truth? Because truth
comes from God, and between man and the truth
there is no merely accidental relationship,
but one that is necessary and essential.

O Jesus, you see the deep desire of my heart
to love you, to become a real minister of yours;
grant me the grace really to do a little good. . . .
(O Jesus, I hope so much from your grace.)

$\mathcal{I}$ shall try hard to foster this devotion [to the Sacred Heart], so that my affectionate and tender feelings for Jesus in the Blessed Sacrament may inspire my whole being, my thoughts, words, and works, and show in all my actions. To do this I need the closest possible union with Jesus, as if I were spending my whole life before his tabernacle. I must think of myself as living solely for the Sacred Heart of Jesus.

$\mathcal{A}$ grave and salutary thought for me:
"I neither fear to die nor refuse to live!
But the life still left in me will be a joyful
preparation for death. I accept death and await
it in confidence—not in myself, for I am a poor
sinner, but in the infinite mercy of the Lord,
to whom I owe all that I am, all that I have.
I will sing of the mercies of God forever."

Prayer

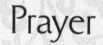

A man of wide reading, meditation,
reflection, and contemplation,
Pope John took advantage of occasions
of public devotion to express the joy of prayer.
He was fond of saying, "The more you pray,
the more you want to pray."

$\mathcal{D}$o not forget your prayers. These may be as short as you wish if you find long prayers too hard, but do not forget them. Even a sign can be a prayer.

$\mathcal{M}$editation [is] never to be omitted (every day); it may be brief if it cannot be longer, but it must be alert, intelligent, and tranquil.

$\mathcal{D}$o not let yourselves be influenced
by the mentality of this world, which finds
no peace because it has forgotten how to pray;
but learn to perfume all your actions with
the life-giving breath of prayer.

$\mathcal{L}$et my familiar prayers be the two
by Saint Ignatius in the book of his *Exercises:*
"Take, O Lord, and receive all my liberty,"
and the other that begins,
"O eternal Creator of all things, I make my oblation."
All my heart is in those two prayers.

✺

$\mathcal{C}$ontinue to follow the fine custom
of offering little flowers of piety. They teach
us to correct our faults, and to become more
attractive in the sight of God and man.

✺

The time I give to active work must be in proportion
to what I give to the work of God, that is, to prayer.
I need more fervent and continual prayer to give character
to my life. So I must give more time to meditation, and
stay longer in the Lord's company, sometimes reading
or saying my prayers aloud or just keeping silent.

$\mathscr{A}$s the foundation of my apostolate, I want an inner
life spent in the search for God in myself and for close
union with him, and in the habitual and tranquil
meditation on the truths that the Church teaches me,
a meditation that, according to the teaching of the
Church, shall be expressed in religious practices
that will become more and more dear to me.

$\mathcal{G}$od is all: I am nothing. Let this do for today.

$\mathcal{T}$he end of life is not complete destruction at death, but rather an immortal life and a homeland that will endure forever. If this teaching, this hope so full of consolation, is stripped from the lives of men, then the whole reason for existence collapses. There is left no checkrein strong enough to bridle the greed, dissension, and discord that try to burst from our very souls.

*S*implicity contains nothing contrary to prudence, and the converse also is true. Simplicity is love: prudence is thought. Love prays: the intelligence keeps watch. "Watch and pray": a perfect harmony.

∽

*L*ord, I need only . . . in this world to know myself and to love you. Give me thy love and thy grace; with these I am rich enough and desire nothing more.

∽

The prayer for peace that rises from the cradle in Bethlehem is a prayer for kindness of heart, for true brotherliness, and for a determination to seek sincere cooperation, rejecting all intrigues and all those destructive elements that we—we repeat— call by their true names: pride, greed, hard-heartedness, and selfishness.

$\mathcal{W}$hen it comes to behavior of ministers, I must
quote for you our predecessor of happy memory,
Pope Pius XII, who rightly observed during one of his
allocutions to the Roman clergy, "If you really desire
that the faithful entrusted to you should pray piously
and ardently, you must be an example to them
in church, and they must see you praying."

The priest who is on his knees before the sacred
tabernacle in a reverent manner, and who prays
attentively to God, is, for the Christian people,
an example offering them an incentive and an
invitation to rival such a priest in zealous piety.

28

Attitudes

❦

*Pope John's daily schedule always
included two periods of examination
of conscience. His was a continuing quest
to enter more and more deeply into
a personal relationship with Christ.
The daily examen always ended with
self-knowledge and a resolve to do better.*

Six Maxims of Perfection

*C*onsidering the purpose of my own life I must:

(1) desire only to be virtuous and holy,
and so be pleasing to God;

(2) direct all things, thoughts as well as actions,
to the increase, the service, and the glory of Holy Church;

(3) recognize that I have been set here by God,
and therefore remain perfectly serene about all that happens,
not only as regards myself, but also with regard to the Church,
continuing to work and suffer with Christ, for her good;

(4) entrust myself at all times to Divine Providence;

(5) always acknowledge my own nothingness;

(6) always arrange my day in an intelligent and orderly manner.

$\mathcal{M}$ankind must be good. This teaching that comes down to us from times long past, and yet speaks to us now in the accents of our own day, reminds all men of their obligation to be good: that is, to be just, righteous, generous, disinterested, ready to understand and to make allowances, willing to show forbearance and forgiveness.

*C*heerfulness at all times, tranquillity, a mind free from care. When I see that I have kept my resolutions carefully, I will praise God from my heart for all he has done; when I have failed, I will be careful not to lose heart and I will think that sometimes God permits this to happen so that I may become more humble and entrust myself more wholly to his loving care.

After any fault, I will make an act of profound humility and then begin again, as cheerfully as ever, smiling as if God had just caressed me, kissed me, and raised me up with his own hands—and I will set out once more, confident, joyful in the name of the Lord!

$\mathcal{W}$e must bear all cheerfully. Our life, especially that part of it that we spend in the company of others, must not be sad and gloomy; we must not let our own boredom, restlessness, and melancholy depress those who are near to us and depend on us. In this life, we have to lift ourselves ever higher. There are various kinds of poetry, but the supreme poetry of this life is found in a joyful soul.

A wise man, a wise Christian, must do all
he can to free himself from sad thoughts, and at
all times have recourse to those sources of comfort
that transform suffering into motives of love,
of merit, of present and eternal joy.

*R*estore to me the joyful certainty that
You will save me: serene confidence in my Savior.
Saint Jerome uses the apt translation "joy of thy Jesus,"
instead of "joy of thy salvation." This is the true joy
of a forgiven soul, the firstfruits of the indwelling
Holy Spirit, to feel numbered with the elect.

The gravest punishment David could impose on his son Absalom, who had betrayed him, was this: "Let him no longer see my face." So we understand why he implores the Lord not to banish him from his sight. It is one thing for God to turn his face away from our iniquities, it is quite another for him to banish the sinner from his sight.

❧

You know that our resignation is neither cowardice nor weakness, but courage and strength. It is founded on God, who sees and hears us wherever we may be and supports us. He enables us to be cheerful and content even when we are under fire, and preserves us from all ill.

❧

*W*e who have faith have no reason to be cast down. We are ready for everything, for every sacrifice.

*T*he keen sense of my own nothingness must ripen and perfect in me the spirit of kindness, making me patient and forbearing with others in the way I judge and treat them. . . . When I feel irritable, I must think of my own unworthiness and of my duty to understand and sympathize with everyone, without passing harsh judgments. This will help me keep calm.

*S*ometimes when you are ill-treated or neglected
you reply with even greater patience and kindness.
This will bring you a great, a very great, blessing.
Be happy and do good . . . and let the sparrows chatter.
This is the best philosophy.

❧

*A*s for the little troubles . . . one must take them
as they come, keep calm and peaceful, and thank
the Lord that they are not worse, and one must
not let one's suffering be seen by others.

❧

*C*harity is a delicate virtue, like chastity. It is easily violated. But those who offend against it assume a grave responsibility and will come to no good. We must follow the old way: speak well of all, suffer for the misfortunes of others, rejoice in their good fortune without envy, forgive, and be patient always. I try to behave in this way, and I am always at peace in my mind.

The first exterior penance that all of us must practice is that of accepting from God, with a resigned and trusting spirit, all the sorrows and sufferings that we encounter in life and those things that involve effort and inconvenience in fulfilling the obligations of our condition in our daily life and the practice of Christian virtue.

*C*harity is indeed the precious gold,
refined in the fire, that enriches all who possess it,
making them the beloved when they disperse it to others.
Whatever you offer . . . without charity will be neither
pleasing to God nor profitable to yourself. . . . You must
have charity, for it surpasses in dignity all other virtues.
May charity set your souls on fire, inspire your souls,
rule your life, and enrich your prayer.

I will be more and more careful to rule my tongue. I must be more guarded in the expression of my opinions, even with persons of my own household.

*F*or my health's sake I must stick to a diet as regards food. I eat little in the evenings already, but now I must eat less at midday too. It will do me good to go out for a walk every day. O Lord, I find this hard and it seems such a waste of time, but still it is necessary, and everybody insists that I should do so. So I shall do it, offering the Lord the effort it costs me.

We must never feel saddened by the very straitened circumstances in which we live; we must be patient, look above, and think of paradise. Paradise, paradise! We shall find our rest there, do you understand? There we shall suffer no more; we shall receive the reward of our works and of our sufferings, if we have borne them with patience.

$\mathcal{I}$ read some passages from Father William Faber, C.O., on kindness. I like this subject because I see that everything is there. I shall go on calmly trying to be, above all, good and kind, without weaknesses, but with perseverance and patience with everyone.

$\mathcal{A}$nyone who judges me from appearance takes me for a calm and steady worker. It is true that I work, but deep in my nature there is a tendency toward laziness and distraction. This tendency, must, with the help of God, be forcibly resisted.

*G*o on living . . . with the Lord's grace in your heart and the sure knowledge that you are pleasing him very much when you do your duty to your country. We are not people to talk or chatter much about these things, as so many idle people do. But we know that our love for our country is none other than our love for our neighbor, and this is all one with the love of God.

I pity those unhappy men who, instead of keeping their sin before them, hide it behind their backs! They will never be free from past or future sins.

$\mathcal{F}$aith and good intentions alone are not enough
to influence a civilization with wholesome principles
and reform it in the spirit of the gospel. For this purpose
it is necessary to penetrate into . . . institutions
and work effectively from within them.

$\mathcal{G}$od created men to be brothers, not enemies.
He gave them the earth to be cultivated in the sweat
of their brow, that everyone might share in its fruits
and take from it the necessities of daily existence.

*T*he Christian style . . . seeks to convince others
with the persuasive power of good manners, and to
attract them with solid arguments, and not by playing on
people's feelings. This sensibility must also be shown in
avoiding exaggerated praise, especially of living people,
and in not attributing all merit to one particular party
or organization, but in knowing how to find something
uplifting in every place or situation, in order to
encourage and to establish fruitful contacts.

*S*uccess is always assured and granted to the humble in heart. The man who has no humility, who yields to the temptations of presumptuous arrogance, is doomed to live bitter days, to find himself before long empty-handed, and to live years of great unhappiness.

*T*he Lord's will is our peace. My episcopal motto: "Obedience and Peace." And we need a spirit of humility and meekness. Believe me, here lies our strength. The Sacred Heart of Jesus is always telling us that this is what we must learn from him: meekness and humility of heart.

Unhappily during the centuries the seamless
robe of Christ has been torn, and is still rent. . . .
It is our duty to soften this discord with our behavior
and our speech, with the example of our humility
and charity—with these two virtues above all,
for they overcome all resistance.

God's power and his love for Holy Church
have not changed with the passing of the centuries.
Even now, where he finds simplicity, humility,
and true love, he still scatters his miracles, which
are not really miracles at all, but the ordinary
responses of divine charity to our own trustful love.

$\mathcal{I}$n our poor life on earth there are two pitfalls: the first is when we are tempted to consider our dwelling place here below as if it were eternal, and the second is that even when we have found a suitable place, we find so much to be grouchy about—trifles and drawbacks and difficulties.

$\mathcal{I}$ live in the midst of wealth and I remain poor;
I receive honors, but my greatest honor is that I was born
poor and reared a Christian, that I received a priestly
vocation, and that I have always preserved the spirit of
simplicity, the simplicity of the countryside of Sotto il
Monte and of the humble family to which I belong, and of
which I am proud. Our honor consists, and must consist,
in our effort to live holy lives without working any
miracles but with the intention of pleasing the Lord.

*B*e true to these words: simplicity and order.
Let all you do be natural and spontaneous without
any affectation, and look always to our Lord Jesus,
who reads your heart and wants you just as you are.

I shall be what the Lord wants me to be.
It is hard for me to think of a hidden life, neglected,
perhaps despised by all, known to God alone.
This is repugnant to my pride. And yet, until I succeed
in doing such violence to my own likes and dislikes
that this obscurity becomes not only indifferent
but welcome and enjoyable, I shall never do
what God wants from me.

$\mathcal{S}$ometimes we think we can solve in all sorts of ways the ordinary problems and difficulties of our lives. We have recourse to complicated and even to difficult means, forgetting that just a little patience is required to arrange everything in perfect order and restore calm and serenity. . . . The Christian must trust the virtue of patience with constant and loving care, until it has become a real and excellent habit, which will result in many advantages and generous rewards.

$\mathcal{T}$here is no learning or wealth, there is no human power, that is more effective than a good nature, a heart that is gentle, friendly, and patient.

Saints

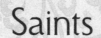

For Pope John it is not enough to be baptized and to go to church. The essence of the Christian vocation is to enter into the mystery of Jesus—to be holy. In short, life is all about being a saint!

What is a saint? Recent distortions have tended to spoil our conception of the saints; they have been tricked out and colored with certain garish tints, which might perhaps be tolerated in a novel, but which are out of place in the real world and in practical life.

To deny oneself at all times, to suppress, within oneself and in external show, all that the world would deem worthy of praise, to guard in one's own heart the flame of a most pure love for God, far surpassing the frail affections of this world, to give all and sacrifice all for the good of others, and with humility and trust, in the love of God and of one's fellowmen, to obey the laws laid down by Providence and follow the way that leads chosen souls to the fulfillment of their mission—and everyone has his own mission— this is holiness, and all holiness is but this.

$\mathscr{A}$s if enraptured by the infinite generosity
of God, Saint Robert Bellarmine asserts that whoever
draws near the most high God with a frank and
open heart may obtain grace and salvation.

$\mathscr{T}$o learn to obey, to learn to keep silence,
to speak when need arises with moderation and
courtesy—this is what Saint Joseph teaches us.

Saint Joseph speaks very little, but he lives intensely, and never seeks to evade any responsibility placed on him by the will of God. He sets us an appealing example of obedience to the divine commands, of serenity at all times, and of perfect trust in God, attained through a life of superhuman faith and charity and, above all, through that great means: prayer.

While his announcement of the Redemption to come was the great glory of John the Baptist's mission, his final witness, given with the sacrifice of his life, confirms his indomitable loyalty to God and to his laws.

To Christ Jesus the glory. He is truly to be "admired in his saints," and supremely admired in Saint Ignatius of Loyola. First of all, Saint Ignatius teaches us not to fear for the Holy Church of Christ, for the Lord sustains her, and preserves in her the very fountain of life, of the apostolate, and of its success.

I like to repeat what the Blessed Gregory Barbarigo used to say so often: "The Lord blesses the cooking pots when they are large." You must have no doubts about the Lord's blessing and his providence, and you must not lie awake sleepless, thinking about what may happen in the future.

$\mathcal{T}$he faith of a humble woman, Martha, was considered worthy to represent the faith of all mankind in Christ the Savior.

The figure of the apostle Paul, with his bold spirit, and his body tempered and worn to the limit of physical endurance, makes a special appeal to all, but particularly to the young, who are naturally generous, impulsive, prone to enthusiasms, and eager to imitate those they admire. In fact, in his epistles, Saint Paul is seen to be very familiar with the striking athletic contests of his day, drawing from them striking examples to illustrate the loftiest moral truths.

For the meaning of ministry, we can but quote the wise words of Saint Pius X, which add force: "For the promotion of the kingdom of Jesus Christ in the world, nothing is more necessary than the holiness of ecclesiastics, that they may give leadership to the faithful by example, by words, and by teaching." This agrees with what Saint John Vianney said in the presence of his bishop: "If you want the entire diocese to be converted to God, then all the parish priests must become saints."

*W*e are sinners and God has forgiven us; he still forgives us and is willing to go on doing so. We feel his presence as a source of constant interior peace, of Christian joy.

$\mathcal{I}$n Catholic tradition, devotion to the saints
is not merely a mark of respect or a brief prayer
on certain occasions, which seem to grow fewer as
life proceeds, but a deeply felt spiritual communion,
an attentive study of the precious examples and lessons
that the saints give us to cheer and encourage us.
"Thy saints, O Lord, will give thee glory."

*E*very one of us has heard and still hears,
ringing in his conscience, the command
"Climb higher," higher, ever higher, until while
we are still on this earth we can reach up to grasp
the heavens, until we can join our saints—
whether they be the venerable saints of old
or the wonderful saints of modern times,
who were our own contemporaries.

Ministry

*The apostolic ministry of
Pope John included several elements
of prayer, service, and devotion
to the will of God.*

T am not going to be a priest just to please someone else, or to make money, or to find comfort, honors, or pleasures. God forbid! It is simply because I want to be able later on to be of some service to poor people, in whatever way I can be.

The priest receives ordination so that he may serve at the altar, and as he has begun the performance of his ministry with the Eucharistic Sacrifice, it follows that the same Eucharistic Sacrifice remains, for the minister of God, as long as he lives, the principle and the source both of the sanctity that he acquires for himself and of the apostolic activity to which he has given himself.

The world has no longer any
fascination for me. I want to be all and
wholly for God, penetrated with his light,
shining with love for God and the souls of men.

❧

Honor is also a great responsibility,
and the man who rises to a certain height
is more likely to fall than the man
who stays on the ground.

❧

*U*nity in prayer, and in the active participation in the celebration of the divine mysteries in the Church's liturgy, contributes in an especially effective way to the wealth of Christian life of both the individual and the community. It is furthermore a marvelous means of education in that charity that is the distinctive sign of the Christian: a charity that is alien to every social, linguistic, and racial discrimination, that stretches its arms and its heart out to all, whether enemies or brothers.

$\mathcal{L}$et us never forget that the principal form
of Eucharistic prayer is never completed and summed
up in the Eucharistic Sacrifice of the altar. . . .
It must especially be kept in mind that the priest,
if he seriously intends, wills, and works to be holy,
must find his model and his heavenly strength
in the Eucharistic Sacrifice he offers.

*E*ven after the much-desired triumph of social justice, there will always remain a wide margin for charity to the poor. . . . For help given to the poor, the Lord reserves his special blessings: the grace of forgiveness and the treasures of his mercy.

*T*here is nothing more noble and more edifying than dying poor, and doing good to others even in the act of dying.

When we remember that to do the will of God in all things and to obey him in a docile spirit, not as if constrained but with a willing heart, constitutes all that is best and finest in life, we can desire nothing else!

∽

The secret of my ministry is in that crucifix you see opposite my bed. It's there so that I can see it in my first waking moment and before going to sleep. It's there, also, so that I can talk to it during the long evening hours. Look at it, see it as I see it. Those open arms have been the program of my pontificate: they say that Christ died for all, for all. No one is excluded from his love, from his forgiveness.

Family

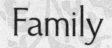

*Pope John loved his family
and confided his most personal
thoughts to them. His sisters, brothers,
nieces, and nephews were his closest
companions and his great comfort.
The ordinariness of family life
is a sanctuary of grace.*

If the Lord should wish me to be the first
of our family to die, I should be quite willing to go,
but if I had to be present at the death of any one of you,
then it would be my greatest consolation at least to
see you die with the tranquil conscience of the just.
For this reason I shall never cease to tell you all:
the pride and boast of our family must be a Christian life
after the old pattern, Christian in church and Christian
also at home in all your personal relationships.

Misunderstandings are by no means rare
even in families—and cause many tears to flow.
But faith is here to show us that if God has
permitted us to suffer, he will help us endure.

The will of God, the will of God—that is enough.
Thank the Lord for what he has given us—I mean,
to me and to all my family—that is enough. The will
of God is our peace and also our perfect joy.

When you feel that your longing for something
is too keen and is causing you pain, then give up
all thought of it and abandon yourselves effortlessly
to the will of God. We are like wayfarers in the world—
some arrive early and some late. We often have to
change our train or coach, or our traveling companions.
We grieve over these partings, but the Lord blesses
them and turns them to good account. What matters
is that sooner or later we arrive at our goal.

$\mathcal{I}$ have never wished or implored from heaven for my family the good things of this world—wealth, pleasures, success—but rather that you should all be good Christians, virtuous and resigned in the loving arms of divine Providence, and living at peace with everyone.

The good fight for the faith is fought not only within the secrecy of the conscience or in the intimacy of the home, but also in public life in all its forms.

Old Age

*Throughout his entire pontificate,
Pope John made continued reference
to the paradox of his very energetic
ministry while enfeebled by his years.
The overall impression he gave is
that old age itself is a vocation.
One cannot make it happen.
God calls you to it, for his purposes.*

*Y*ou must respect the old, and during the years of youth and maturity you must be generous in service to God. In this way we can be sure that the young people of today will enjoy a serene and trustful old age, strengthened by fine memories of the good they have done.

The older I grow, surrounded by worldly greatness and honor, the more I feel drawn to the greatest *simplicity*, in giving as in receiving, in joy as in grief, with trust in the Lord who enables us to see everything clearly, and in the effort to avoid any excessive pleasure or sorrow.

My own personal serenity, which makes
such an impression on people, derives from this:
the obedience in which I have always lived, so that
I do not desire or beg to live longer, even a day beyond
that hour in which the Angel of Death will come
to call me and take me, as I trust, to paradise.

*O*ld age, . . . a great gift of the Lord's, must be for me a source of *tranquil inner joy*, and a reason for trusting day by day in the Lord himself, to whom I am now turned as a child turns to his father's open arms.

$\mathcal{W}$e must always treat elderly people with great respect and affectionate care. They possess a real treasure of gifts and graces that the Lord has showered on them on the long way they have come, and this treasure will be of priceless value to them when they reach the end of their earthly pilgrimage.

Mary: Mother of God

———◁◁◁———

Pope John's favorite shrine was Lourdes.
He had first gone there in 1905, when appointed
secretary to his own bishop, Monsignor James
Radini-Tedeschi. Every year of his tenure as
nuncio in France, he made a pilgrimage there.
He consecrated the new basilica at Lourdes
while patriarch of Venice. John's Marian
devotion is a hallmark of his spirituality.

The daily Eucharistic procession in the afternoon at Lourdes is simply the reenactment of the passing of the living Jesus through the midst of the crowds, to teach them and grant them miracles and graces of all kinds. So the visit to our Lord in these places is like a renewal of faith, adoration, and love for Jesus, the true center of Catholic liturgy, as of Catholic life.

❧

In Mary's company, age does not wither us; everyone may keep the freshness and charm of childhood, which induced a great writer to comment, "Nothing can be lovelier than a child reciting the Hail Mary!"

❧

The sweet memory of our young years
has never left us with the passing of time nor
has it weakened. It has helped—and we say this
with paternal confidence—to make the holy
rosary very dear to our soul, and we never
fail to recite it in its entirety every day.

Christian life is sacrifice. Through self-sacrifice
inspired by love, we share in that which was the
final purpose of the earthly life of Jesus, who became
our brother, sacrificed himself, and died for us in
order to ensure for us, through his human life,
our joy and glory in eternity.

*C*hristian piety has rejoiced to learn from the book of Acts that Mary was present at the first gatherings of the faithful, when they broke bread together as brothers and spent long hours in prayer. . . . When we say that in the Eucharist we have the Son and in Mary we have his mother, have we not said all?

O Mary, Mary, we beg from you holiness of life, because this is what matters most on earth and in heaven.

The rosary, as is known to all, is in fact a very
excellent means of prayer and meditation, in the form
of a mystical crown in which the prayers "Our Father,"
"Hail Mary," and "Glory be to the Father" are intertwined
with meditation on the greatest mysteries of our faith,
and which presents to the mind, like so many pictures,
the drama of the Incarnation of our Lord
and the Redemption.

A sign of consent from Mary, the humble maiden of Nazareth, and the mystery is accomplished. From the first cry of the infant Jesus in Bethlehem till his last gasp on Golgotha, the miracle is worked: the fountains of salvation are unsealed, the redemption of mankind is accomplished—peace is assured to men of goodwill. And with peace comes grace, every boon of heaven and earth; the gates are opened to that eternity of bliss so ardently desired by every living soul here below.

$\mathcal{T}$he doctrine about the body of the blessed Virgin Mary
being preserved by the Holy Trinity from all corruption,
and immediately transfigured and spiritualized, . . .
exalts the eternal values of the spiritual world, with
its intrinsic needs and irrepressible aspirations.

It renews our hope of a happier future.

It restores our faith in a more perfect justice,
which will reestablish the order disturbed by sin.

Finally, it restores hope, which turns the
bitterness and hardship of life into joy.

Mary is with us, among us;
she protects and helps us;
she leads us along a sure road.

The Cross of Christ

⸻

Pope John's close collaborators, and even the participants of the Second Vatican Council, could not but notice the frequency of his mention of the Cross and its value. A crucifix was his constant companion. His personal theology of the Cross seems to be derived from the writings of Saint John Vianney and also the fathers of the Church. He saw it not as an instrument of torture but as a sign of victory, in order that the Church would "shine with glory!"

$\mathcal{M}$y present: Here I am then, still alive in my sixty-ninth year, prostrate over the crucifix, kissing the face of Christ and his sacred wounds, kissing his heart, laid bare to his pierced side; here I am showing my love and grief.

How could I not feel grateful to Jesus, finding myself still young and robust of body, spirit, and heart?

*F*ollowing in the footsteps of apostolic men of all times, he [St. John Vianney] realized very well that it was through the Cross that he could work most effectively for the salvation of those who had been confided to his care. For their sake and without complaint he suffered calumnies, prejudices, and adversities of every sort. For their sake he willingly bore the most painful vexations of mind and body which accompanied the daily administration of the Sacrament of Penance, which was almost never interrupted over the course of thirty years. For their sake he, as an athlete of Christ, fought against diabolical enemies. For their sake, finally, he brought his body into subjection by voluntary mortification. On this point, there is his answer to that priest who had complained to him that his own apostolic zeal had brought forth no fruits: "Have you prayed to God? Have you wept? Have you cried out in pain? Have you sighed? Have you also fasted, going without proper sleep, and sleeping on the bare floor? Until you have done these things, do not imagine that you have made every effort."

*H*ow true it is that the Lord wants
us all for himself and for that life which
will have no end, and which we cannot
earn without bearing our cross.

*E*ven if he lays on our shoulders some part
of his own cross, he is there to help us
bear it with self-sacrifice and with love.

There is only one truth, and it is always the same, the truth of the gospel: We must learn to forget and forgive, to render good for evil, always remembering the words of Jesus on the cross: "Father, forgive them, for they know not what they are doing."

Nothing is dearer to the Lord, who suffered so much for us, than our imitation of him in suffering and silence. But the silence must be absolute and observed with everyone, and the suffering must be accepted willingly for the love of Jesus.

The life of men is a pilgrimage, continual, long, and wearisome. Up and up along the steep and stony road, the road marked out for all on that hill. In this mystery, Jesus represents the whole race of men. Every one of us must have his own cross to bear, otherwise, tempted by selfishness or cruelty, we should sooner or later fall by the roadside.

From the contemplation of Jesus climbing up to Calvary we learn, first with our hearts and then with our minds, to embrace and kiss the cross and bear it bravely and with joy, as we read in *The Imitation of Christ*: "In the cross is our salvation, in the cross is our life, in the cross is our defense against our foes, and our heavenly sweetness."

In this life, there is nothing better than bearing my cross, as Jesus sets it on my shoulders and on my heart. I must think of myself as the man bearing the cross, and love the cross that God sends me without thinking of any other. All that is not to the honor of God, the service of the Church, and the welfare of souls is extraneous to me, and of no importance.

*K*now that the *practice of patience* means first of all rejecting the frivolous pleasures of the world and always cherishing in our hearts the commandments of God's Son, with the help of his grace, which is distilled through his most precious blood; and it means receiving in our souls the marks of his passion and indescribable sufferings—a sure sign of great blessing.

$\mathcal{P}$riests often find themselves in difficult situations. There is no reason to be astonished at this, for those who hate the Church attack the priests by troubling them and by laying traps for them. As the Curé of Ars himself said, "Those who want to overthrow religion start out by hating the priest."

The image of the Crucified . . . the sign and the companion of your mission, will remind you of the road you must follow in order to ensure full success for your labors. Christ nailed to the cross, put to death by painful torture, holds out his hands to embrace all men. He will teach you what it costs to save the world. He is the model and example for you to follow. Saint Leo says: "You can reach him only by imitating his patience and his humility. On the road you will have to face fatigue and exhaustion, the clouds of sadness, and the storms of fear."

*E*aster is for us all a dying to sin, to passion,
to hatred and enmity, and all that brings about disorder,
spiritual and material bitterness, and anguish.
This death is indeed only the first step toward a higher
goal—for our Easter is also a mystery of new life.

*T*he resurrection of the Lord truly represents—and
for this reason it is celebrated every year—the renewed
resurrection of every one of us to the true Christian life,
the perfect Christian life that we must all try to live.

I am ready to go. I've said all my breviary and the whole rosary. I've prayed for the children, for the sick, for sinners. . . . Will things be done differently when I'm gone? That's none of my business. I feel joy in the contemplation of truth and duty done. I am glad I was able to correspond to every impulse of grace.

Conclusion

We know a few things about the activities of the future Pope John XXIII on October 25, 1958, the day he entered the conclave that elected him supreme pontiff of the Roman Catholic Church. Early in the morning, he cut himself severely while shaving in his quarters at the residence, Domus Maria. This annoyed him greatly because he rarely, if ever, cut himself shaving. Later, at mass, he remembered in prayer the recent death of his friend Cardinal Celso Constantini, formerly apostolic nuncio in China and a very revered figure of the Roman Curia during the pontificate of Pope Pius XII. Cardinal Constantini had followed Pope Pius XII in death.

At two o'clock in the afternoon, while the rest of Rome sat down to lunch, he assembled with the other cardinal members of the conclave to hear a discourse by then-monsignor Antonio Bacci, the papal Latinist. For all his classical involvement and artistic refinement, Cardinal Bacci gave a remarkable pastoral address, calling for new, functional, and effective lines of communication throughout the entire Church. His homily climaxed with this sentence: "We need a pope who is above all holy, so that he may obtain from God what lies beyond natural gifts." At four o'clock, Vatican officials closed the shutters, doors, and staircases, thus sealing off the conclave from the world, leaving the complex of the Sacred Palace in silence and shadows.

Sometime in the course of that very busy day, the future pope found time to write a letter to Giuseppe Piazzi, bishop of Bergamo and intimate friend of Cardinal Angelo Roncalli. These were the last words that he penned before disappearing into the walls of the Vatican: "My soul is comforted with confidence in the new Pentecost, which will enable us to give a new vigor to the victory of truth, to what is good, and to peace through the renewal of the Head of the Holy Church."

At the beginning of the Second Vatican Council, Pope John called again for a new Pentecost. His faith in the power and direction of the Holy Spirit was total. Perhaps because of that trust, his joyful soul could foresee that the fruit of his activity, inspired and spontaneous, yet consistent, would "shine with glory!"

A Last Message to the World,
Friday, May 24, 1963

Monsignor Capovilla, then the Pope's personal secretary, was one of the group that surrounded John XXIII as he lay dying. He reports that Pope John, with considerable effort, rose to a sitting position and spoke words he had evidently composed and committed to memory some time before. This was his last message, as recorded by Monsignor Capovilla. Pope John XXIII died shortly thereafter, on June 3.

"For the benefit of the entire world, we treat the highest affairs, inspired by the will of the Lord.

"Now, more than ever, more certain than in the past centuries, we are intent on serving humankind as such, not only Catholics defending above all and anywhere the rights of the human being, not only those of the Catholic Church. The present circumstances, the needs of the last fifty years, and doctrinal discussion have led us to new realities, as I said in the opening speech of the Council. It is not that the gospel is changing; we are starting to understand it better. He who has lived longer and found himself at the beginning of the century facing new duties in a social activity investing all of man, he who has been, as I, twenty years in the East, eight in France, and has been able to compare different cultures and traditions, knows that the moment has come to acknowledge *the signs of the times,* to capture the opportunities and look afar."

Editor's Note

I want to acknowledge, first and foremost, Margaret L. Hoenig, without whom this book could not have been completed. I also thank Father Paul Joseph Fullam, C.P., and Father Xavier Hayes, C.P., for the resources provided. Finally, I express my gratitude to the Most Reverend José Agustín Orbegozo, C.P., Superior General of the Passionists, for his support and his presence.

The selection of the texts contained herein results from much consultation with persons associated with Pope John XXIII during his pontificate, and the arrangement of themes comes as a result of their consensus. Most helpful among this support group were Cardinal Achille Silvestrini, Cardinal William Baum, and Archbishop Loris Capovilla.